PEREGRINATIONS OF THE WORDSMITH

A second book of verse

Ted Morgan

First published (Paperback) in the UK in 2016
by Violet Circle Publishing.
Manchester, England, UK.
ISBN: 978-1-910299-18-0

Text Copyright © Ted Morgan 2016.

Cover Photograph "Garlic in the Woods" Ted Morgan 2016
Cover concept and design © Violet Circle Publishing 2016

All rights are reserved: no part of this may be stored in a retrieval system, reproduced or transmitted by any means, electronic, mechanical, photocopying, or otherwise without the prior written permission of the publisher, in accordance with the terms of licenses issued by the Copyright Licensing Agency.

All characters and scenarios in this publication are fictitious and any resemblance to real persons, living or dead is purely coincidental.

British Library Cataloguing in Publication Data.

A catalogue record for this book is available from the British Library.

All papers used in the production of this book are sourced only from wood grown in sustainable forests.

www.violetcirclepublishing.co.uk

This is my second book of verse. All my royalties from it will be donated to the Bolton Hospice. My first book of poems Wordsmith Wanderings has raised a tidy sum for this very worthy cause and I hope this volume will do the same.

My poems reflect the many facets of nature and life, some sad, some descriptive of modern life and its problems, both serious and funny. My warped sense of humour will be evident in some and I apologise in advance for this aspect of my personality.

I hope you will enjoy this volume and by purchasing it you will have helped to raise money for a very worthy cause which cared for my late wife with such care and compassion in the final days of her life.

Dedicated to
Ann Redburn
A true friend

True Friendship is often sought but seldom found,

It has the capacity to enrich our lives,

To support us when times are bad,

To give clarity to us when things are confused,

A true friend does all of these things,

Without judgment, malice or spite,

They walk with us and support us

Through all of life's tribulations,

They rejoice with us at our successes,

When we find a true friend let us treasure them.

Contents

Peregrination	1
Early Morning	2
Morning Thoughts	3
Bluebells	5
Daffodils	6
Mists	7
Lament for Lahore	9
The Jobsworth	10
Trout Fishing	11
Rainbow	12
Two Years	13
Sitting	14
St. George's Day	15
Arthur Ransome's Books	16
Ode from a Confused Lancastrian	18
Nurse Training in the early 1960's	19
My Hearing	23
My European View	24
Dire Here	26
Computer Crazy	28
Agatha Dewdrop	29
Canadian Confusion	31
Reverie	33
Sparky	34
Tinkerbelle's House	36
The Joys of Motoring	37
The Fair	39
Phone Call	40
Radio	41
Woodlands Song	42
Orange	43

Number 13......44
Mortality......45
Light......46
Mi Sisters Boyfriend......47
Golfing Jeff......49
Farewell......52
Halloween Night......53
Invictus......55
With thanks to the Battle of Britain Pilots......56
The Cross in Town......57
Alberts Surprise......58
Christmas Markets......60
Isolation......61
Autumn Morning......62
A Christmas Message......63
Birds......64
The local......65
Christmas Feast......67
Eagles......68
The Haggis Hunt......69
Christmas Floods......71
Vandals......73
Thought Block......74
Spending......75
Mothering Sunday......76
What's in a Name?......77
Iona's Friend......78
Wee Folk......79
Woodland Magic......80
Depression......81
Rain......82
Edgar Einstein......84
"Lucky " Smith......85

Definition:-Peregrination to travel from one place to another

Peregrination

Wordsworth wandered as a cloud,
Through daffodils beside a lake,
And ramblers wander on the hills,
Midst bogs and moors causing muscle ache,
Whilst the country lanes of England's shires,
Give vistas that we all admire,
The smells and sounds of country life,
Uplift the soul and lessen strife,
But a friend of mine (who knows big words)
Came out with one I had not heard,
He said to me "Go peregrinate"
It caused me to wonder what's my fate.
I had to find out mighty quick,
Just in case that I was sick,
Then looking into hefty tome,
I did just that, I wandered home.

Early Morning

I rise from bed each morning, with sleep coating my eyes,
And stagger to the kitchen, where the coffee pot doth lie,
My bloods pressure is way too high or so the doctor says,
So tablets two I have to take or mend my lifestyle ways,
Then off to the bathroom for a wash with flannel blue,
Grab a brush, clean my teeth, use the loo, and sip my brew,
In the shower feel all clean, wash my hair to impart a sheen,
Look in mirror what a sight, give myself a morning fright,
Looking now all neat and spry, smelling nice, glint in eye,
I get dressed in lounging gear, no posh designer labels here,
Now morning news on radio four,
Sit down in chair to snooze once more!

We all wake up and just daydream at times often we use this time to think about our life, this poem does encapsulate our random thought at this time.

Morning Thoughts

It's dark when you wake in the morning,

The sun is nowhere around,

You lie in your bed and you listen,

Hear nothing but clock's ticking sound,

It's then that you start thinking,

And ideas run round in your brain,

All the ifs and maybes of past times,

And paths taken you cannot change,

'If only' is never a good start,

When you lie there and your life recall,

It's never the good that you cherish,

It's mistakes that you made that appal,

Dark mornings are never a good time,

To straighten the crooked path of life,

Wait for the birds mooring chorus,

To herald the end of your strife,

The warmth of the sun and the birdsong,

Stir the soul to happier times,

And you recall times spent with a loved one,

Maybe in sunnier climes,

So try and wake up in the morning,

With a smile to greet the new day,

And remember the good that you did,

As you travelled down life's long pathway,

So on waking each morning, greet the day with a smile,

Challenge the new day ahead,

And leave negative thoughts behind you,

As you spring from your nice comfy bed.

Bluebells

Into the woods I strolled, on a springtime sunlit day,

And beneath the trees so tall, was a wondrous blue display,

In large and spreading clusters,

And peeping out from grassy banks,

Were gently swaying Bluebells in tightly clustered ranks,

The woods bedecked in colour, made my heart just soar,

For the scene laid out before me filled the forest floor,

In books the flower of the Bluebell is used for fairy's caps,

Whilst tiny woodland dwellers search for pollen and for snacks,

Bees search each new flower, so that honey can be made,

And I just gaze in wonder, at this magic woodland glade.

Daffodils

A mass of yellow you can see,

Across the fields and midst the trees,

Peeping out with springtime pride,

Neath tangled bush that tries to hide,

Their yellow heads which sway in time,

A springtime herald whilst in their prime,

A brief display we know so well,

Sadly they'll soon say farewell,

But daffodils sprung from winters cold,

Display a glowing heart of gold,

We see with joy their spring display,

The sight of which makes our day.

The moors of the Lancashire Pennines surround my hometown and I have been wandering in the hills on many occasions when the mists descended. These are my thoughts on this.

Mists

The hoarfrost drapes the frozen ground,

In a cloak of shimmering crystal hues,

Swirling mists obscure

Views of the distant mountain scene,

Like sentries, the shrouded trees bedecked

In winter's leafless pose, appear and disappear

Creeping cloud of mists and fog passes silently by,

No sound is heard, no birdsong,

Disturbs this eerie ethereal world,

As silently you wander, cut off, aloof,

Yet clad in mist yourself,

You become part of this lifeless,

Silent, and invisible landscape,

In life at times, we emulate,

This lifeless, silent world,

We sometime cut ourselves off

From other people's view,

And enter a world, which only we have access to,

Within our being we wander through the mists of memories,

Half-forgotten events, clouded by the mists of time

Our journey of recollection mirrors a walk

In mist bedecked moorland,

Alone, apart,

Yet part of the landscape of life,

But when the winds come to drive away the clouds and mists,

Like our memories they are revealed in all their beauty and colour.

Like many people I was shocked and saddened by the massacre of children and people in a terrorist bomb attack on a fair during the 2016 Easter holiday in Lahore India.

Lament for Lahore

A pleasant Sunday in a city far away

Children enjoying the Easter holiday,

A loud report then devastation reigns,

A mother weeping over her child's remains,

Why this barbaric act? Why these infant deaths?

Hear no excuse for this perverted act in religions name,

It kills Christians, Muslims, Hindus and Jews,

They are people just the same as you,

These twisted misguided bombers, espousing religious war,

God's children killed in a war on God.

Having worked within the public service I have on occasions come across the odd Jobsworth character I cannot help but do this tongue in cheek ode

The Jobsworth

All the councils have a jobsworth of that I'm very sure.
He walks around the borough in a garb you can't ignore,
Polished shoes and smart peaked cap,
A scarf and gloves to match,
With the council logo emblazoned on his hat,
With his little book and pencil, he writes notes as you pass by,
You wonder what he writes about, he is the council spy,
He peers around the corners, and into refuse bins,
To see that regulations are not broken,
By what's enclosed within,
He follows doggie walkers, to catch them unawares,
No poo on the pavements, or on the council squares,
Buskers in the market square he quickly moves them on,
If they do not have a permit,
Signed or stamped by Town Clerk John,
He's puffed up with importance, his nose up in the clouds,
His bearings high and mighty, his voice is rather loud,
A tiny man with attitude, in a job he thinks is grand,
A pretentious little lackey of Red Tape Council Land.

Trout Fishing

You view the expanse of water, your heart starts beating fast,

In anticipation of the day ahead,

As you see trout go swimming past,

You have your tackle ready and a box that's full of flies,

Your rod and line are in your hand,

As you seek that elusive prize,

You hear the swish of fly line as you cast it far from shore,

And hope that the fly which lands, has that fatal fish allure,

You slowly pull towards you that brightly coloured line,

With the fly upon the leader,

On which you hope the fish will dine,

Many casts later, and still no takes in sight,

But you vow to keep on trying till evening turns to night,

But after all the waiting, your fly disappears,

And a screaming reel does tell you

that your quarry has appeared,

You fight the frenzied acrobat as he tries to slip the hook

It twists and turns and gives a fight, before it's brought to book,

You dispatch it quickly as your priest says it's amen,

And with dinner in your creel, you begin to fish again.

Rainbow

It is said that gold is found at every rainbow's end,
And rain soaked clouds reflect the peeping rays of the sun
Upon the multi-coloured falling drops of rain,
We gaze in wonder at the scope of the colours shown,
It's one of nature's odes to earthly beauty,
It shines for such a short time; and then is gone,
With only our minds eye to remember
The beauty of the scene

This was written on the second anniversary of my wife's death.

Two Years

Its two years now since she passed on,
It's hard to say just how I feel,
The memories they linger on,
At times I really think they're real,
Its little things that stir the mind,
You remember times when things are found,
A ring, a clip, a silly toy you bought,
Which gave her so much joy,
The emptiness I feel within,
Compounds at times to emphasise my loss,
This is when I feel bereft,
Caused by my loving partners death,
But still I play my part each day,
A smile to people as I go on my way,
As I am sure other people find,
Their loss is still within their mind,
It's hard to shake away these thoughts,
Which leave you feeling so distraught,
Time eases pain or so I'm told,
But its slow movement as you grow old,
Gives you time to contemplate,
The joy that together in each other found
And a love that truly knew no bounds.

This poem was started on the 20th of November 2013 as I sat by my wife Pat's bedside In the Bolton Hospice. The first four lines were written on my tablet, she died the day after they were written and I found them some months later and finished the poem.

Sitting

I sit here in the hospice at the bedside of my wife,
Sun shines through the window as she battles for her life,
Sitting here seeing her, tears my heart in two,
But I can only sit here, there's nothing I can do,
I watch as she fights the last battle of her life,
And I sit feeling helpless, doing nothing to ease her plight,
The place it is so tranquil so silent and serene,
But to me it is a battlefield with cancer as the fiend,
I never thought that we would part in such a place as this,
We did not know our destiny we thought our life was bliss,
I sit here and contemplate the life that we had had,
So many very good time that were tempered by some bad,
The love and happiness that we had, will last for evermore,
But the loss I felt when she had gone,
Cut my heart right to its core,
We all have to face the loss of someone very dear,
No longer to have their presence, no longer have them near,
How we'll cope no one can tell, that path we tread alone,
But it's a journey we all must take, and we do it on our own.

St. George's Day

We celebrate St. Georges Day on March the twenty Third,

But unfortunately for most folks, the date is never heard,

We English should be oh so proud, of our past and heritage,

But it seem to me that patriotism is from a bygone age,

Its way past time we had a change, and St. George we celebrate,

To let the other nations know, that we are not so second rate,

Step out with pride in red and white, on a banner with a cross

And proclaim to one and all that our cause is far from lost,

So celebrate St George's day, so everyone can see,

That English pride is still alive and to non we bend a knee.

As a young boy I rushed home from school to listen to Pigeon Post read in instalments on the children's hour on the BBC home service. I have been entranced by this author ever since and even now at 78 I still have all Arthur Ransome's books on my shelf. This poem was published in the Arthur Ransome Society's magazine this year.

Arthur Ransome's Books

Peter Duck and Pigeon Post, Amazons and Swallows,
Some of the books from my youth,
In my heart I'll always follow,
Adventures in the Lake District
With John, Susan and their Craft,
With Titty and boy Roger and all their stores stowed aft,
Whilst Nancy and mate Peggy crewed Amazon their boat,
Would terrorise their uncle Jim and raid his home afloat,
Off in search of treasure in the surrounding hills and fells,
Whilst mining what they thought was gold
Was a dream to which they held,
The North Pole was their aim when ice covered all the lake,
And in Winter Holiday Dot and Dick made a great mistake,
Their wind powered sledge on ice it sped,
Until the weather changed,
They had no idea they were alone and were in fact estranged,
Battling through a snowstorm, too soon to win the race,

They got to the North Pole but saw no friendly face,
Adventures off in foreign climes whilst meeting Missee Lee,
And a very foggy journey in We Didn't Mean to Go to Sea,
The Norfolk Broads and Scotland
feature in Arthur Ransome's tales,
With boats and nature both entwined
Which you can now avail,
So go and read a Ransome book no matter what your age,
You will enjoy it I am sure be you junior or sage.

Ode from a Confused Lancastrian

I'm told I come from Greater Manchester
The Town Hall politicians have said,
That's funny I thought my mum said to me
That I was Lancashire bred,
It seems to me a muck up
That's left be bewildered and sad,
I thought I was brought up in Lancashire
When I was just a wee lad,
They have gone and changed all the boundaries
And Lancashire to me is no more,
I'm told I'm a Greater Mancunian
That title can go through the door,
I'm a Lancastrian Lad and I'm proud that I am,
And whatever them fools want to say,
The Red Rose of Lancashire will be on my chest
Until my dying day,
So that's settled and nothing will change it,
No matter how much they rave,
For Bolton and Lancashire will be in my breast,
To the day I go to my Grave.

I have nursed in the RAF and am qualified in General Nursing (SRN) and also Psychiatric Nursing (RMN)

The following poem Is a rather tongue in cheek tale of my training at Bolton General hospital and my initial training at Withington Hospital, all the incidents did take place! Honest

Nurse Training in the early 1960's

I went into the training school as I thought I'd be a nurse,

My mind was full of high ideals good sense was in reverse,

In swept the Sister Tutor like a ship with billowed sales

She then started to tell us how we should cut our nails,

Hair it was better, if kept short and out of sight,

And even to us males in class she regaled us with her likes,

We had eight weeks study, where we practiced on each other,

We did not get near patients, for that caused too much bother,

Injections were all practiced on a nearby handy orange

To do so on each other hurt too much and made us cringe,

Anatomy was taught, lurid pictures, bits of bones,

And every notch and pointy bit, each in separate zones,

Each nurse had to make, an extract called Beef Tea

But mine it just boiled away,

Which caused much merriment and glee,

The sister tutor she did frown and her face it went bright red,
She said that all male nurses "were so much better dead"
Our visit to the sewage works was part of hygiene's course,
And an enthusiastic worker
showed us round its large concourse,
The smell it was atrocious, with swirling tanks and drains,
And large rotating sprinklers like propellers seen on planes,
The off with the health inspectors, to visit shops and pubs,
Visit "grotty"houses and even "grotty clubs",
District nurses took us to see patients in their homes
To the patients they were angels,
Especially those who lived alone,
The scope of work was massive
And it made us catch our breath,
To be part of this endeavour seeing life and even death,
We worked so hard at learning, all aspects of our calling,
We found the work was tiring but never once was boring,
Eight weeks after "into "block they let us loose on wards,
Filled with nursing knowledge on unsuspecting patient hoards,
The Staff Nurse was our teacher the Sister she was God,
And woe betide the student who forgot this,
When on her ward they trod!

I learn so many things, at times I'd stand and gawk,

But Sister she was everywhere with the eyesight of a hawk,

And it was to me that she did shout,

"That's not Right" and "Who did this?"

Ward experience for me was far from nursing bliss,

I then did the unthinkable put flowers Red with White,

I did not know that it was taboo,

And was banished from Sisters sight,

At six months we had a test of the knowledge we had learned,

And sat several written papers

Which had most of us concerned,

Ward practice and school study, made time just seem to fly,

When at twelve months exam's again, I did not feel so spry,

On looking at the questions my mood was one of gloom,

I was tense and apprehensive as I sat there in that room,

But I did pass the Part Two tests and I felt I walked on air,

I had survived the first twelve months

Despite moments of despair,

Experience in the specialties was trauma for us all,

The sight and sounds of daily care

And at patient's beck and call,

Night duty it was hard at first a strange ethereal world,

So much to do, so little time, as round the ward you whirled,

The early morning was a rush, all washed by half past six.

Serve the breakfast,

Straighten beds before day staff joined the mix,

Casualty and minor op's was where we learnt our poise,

Seeing lots of nasty accidents to little girls and boys,

Ophthalmic was a mystery and E.N.T. the same,

But slowly we gained the knowledge

That fanned our nursing flame,

We shouldered responsibility, our confidence it grew,

And after another two long years of graft,

Our finals we went through,

Our untold joy when we passed it really knew no bounds,

State Registered Nurse, now that thought to me it still astounds.

Ted Morgan SRN RMN.

Continually turning up the sound on the T.V got me in hot water many times so off I went to have my hearing checked.

My Hearing

I thought I'd have my hearing checked,
Some words I seem to miss,
So off I went to the hearing shop, to hear all sounds is bliss,
The man he put me in a booth with headphones on "mi bonce"
He said that when I heard a sound to press a button once,
Some sounds I heard right away I felt this was a doddle,
But when the man showed me my test results
Hearing's in a muddle
With low sound I had no problem, but as up the scale I went,
It seemed to him the higher sounds,
Proved my hearing pitchforks, bent,
He said that he could fix it with two space age bits of kit,
Then sent me down to smart dressed girls
My hearing aids to fit,
Two tiny little gadgets were fitted in my ears,
Then hooked me to a lap top to test what I could hear,
The results they were amazing I can hear what people say,
All the good words and the bad words that go to make my day,
They did not cost a penny as the government paid the bill,
It came about because I thought, my hearing it was ill.

This was written before the Vote to get out of the European Common Market was taken.

My European View

We joined the common market many years ago,
But we did not then envisage what a monster was to grow,
The politicians told us it was all about free trade,
With our continental cousins
Who would buy the goods we made,
It now seems in the meantime this view got kind of twisted,
It appointed lots of commissioners not elected but enlisted,
Their desks are full I of edicts,
Regulations each country should approve,
They strangle us with "Red Tape"
But our lives they don't improve,
The accounts seem rather "dodgy"
As each year they do not pass,
The auditors say some money has just vanished, is this graft?
The CAP seems good to some but not to all I fear,,
And our fishing fleets have problems
With new Quota's every year,
Some countries call for closer ties, and a federal Europe state,
But patriotic people say that this would just frustrate,
We never voted to join this club, as Europe clearly proves,

But still we pour our money in, to which many disapprove,
Different countries cause a national backlash,
Why don't they ask all people
About this countywide mishmash?
I know that here in Britain my views a bit one sided,
But think on these things when you go and vote
As our country's fate's decided.

I had a bad attack of the "Trots" or "Delhi Belly" and felt moved to write this ode.

Dire Here

He awoke in the dead of night,

His tummy flux did not feel right

He thought, this is dire here,

And to the throne he disappeared,

Trapped though by natures whim,

The fluid it just poured from him,

He cannot leave this seat of care,

Whilst moaning in such great despair,

What if he's trapped here for a week?

His sit upon began to tweak

He felt faint and very flustered,

By this ague germs had mustered,

He could not stop this fluid flow,

That emanated from below,

His vitals he was sure were gone,

Passed quickly via his sit-upon,

Some physic was his need,

To stop this dredful fluid bleed,

But how to get to pharmacist,

He was not such an optimist,

That he had drugs to stem the flow,

Of all that emanated from below,

At last the lava flow did ease,

And to the chemist he did speed,

Some tablets bought with coin of land,

He rushed back home with pills in hand,

And swallowed them with much speed,

Waiting now for his guts to seize,

But alas it was some time,

Before his ague did decline,

For a few more days his guts rebelled,

Whilst gas and fluid were expelled,

Then at last that blessed day,

When all his anguish went away,

For he was healed and walked in peace,

Without his bot being tightly creased!

This poem is dedicated to my Daughter-in –Law Corinne my saviour in all computer matters

Computer Crazy

My computer's going crazy it won't do as it's told,
The internet is on and off I think it's getting old,
My mouse it does not like me, my cursor's in a tizzy,
The darn thing moves around so much,
It makes me feel quite dizzy,
My programs will not open, I think they've gone on strike,
Or else they are on work to rule and open when they like,
I feel my "Puter" is possessed with Worms and Trojan Beasties,
Just to get me mad as hell tearing my hair out in pieces,
What can I do? I'm so bereft, the machine it sits there blinking,
And how to get the darn thing fixed, I have not got an inkling,
I need a computer nerd who takes its kind of language,
One who can make it toe, the line and dissipate my anguish,
I do know such a person who can sort my problem "puter"
Her Mantra is "No Problem"
And her mainframe couldn't be cuter,
So off I take my desk top for her tender ministrations,
I know that she will quell my fears,
And cure my great frustrations,
My Computer now is back on line,
Its curser no longer wanders,
Obeys orders that I type in,
Means it no longer stops and ponders,
I now can calmly type with windows that are lit
That is until the next time my computer throws a fit.

A Halloween nonsense poem

Agatha Dewdrop

Agatha Dewdrop was a witch
With crooked hat and wart on lip,
She used to fly when night time came,
On her broomstick in wind and rain,
But now alas she lies a bed,
With pains in bones and hips instead,
For this is due to damp and wet,
When raincoat she did forget,
For when young and newly trained,
She scoffed at others aches and pains,
And dashed around casting spells,
For lovelorn Shepherds and their belles,
Not thinking of the time when she would age,
Grow old disgracefully,
The fun she had when wild and free,
Scaring people outrageously,
And casting spells in an iron pot,
Above a fire that glowed red hot,

Viper's skin and eye of toad,

Carrion from a blood soaked road

All tossed in pot with herbs and spice,

Put in so it would smell quite nice,

With this potion she caused a stir,

It made the vicars eyesight blur,

It caused him such great distress

As he could not read Sunday's address,

The Doctor had his problems too,

With people's ears full up with goo,

A surgery filled with stone deaf blokes,

Who could not hear him when he spoke,

At Halloween Agatha's illness struck,

Her sister witches ran amok,

Arthritis caused her hips to stick,

She could not mount her big broomstick,

Her pills and potions would not shift,

The pain and stiffness in her hips,

Remember that you should all wrap up,

Lest you like Agatha in bed are stuck

My late wife had many relatives in Canada and dedicate this to them for their help in teaching me to speak a "new language".

Canadian Confusion

My first trip to Canada had me all confused

The words are all in English,

But they're not the words I used,

It seems I ride the elevator, but to me it's still a lift,

But the pavement is the sidewalk,

I'm getting the lingo's drift,

When it comes to where one lives, a sub-division is its name

But here in good old England an estate seems rather tame,

When I walk towards a car,

Parts have all been changed

The boot is now the trunk or so it has been named,

The fender is the bumper; the chrome it gleams and shines,

And they seem to have more gadgets

that I have ever seen on mine,

To access the engine means I have to raise the hood,

They drive the cars on the roads wrong side;

That's not to me so good,

And when we get to eating, confusion reigns supreme
A courgette is a zucchini,
And they eat no lamb it seems,
When I ask for some chips,
A packet of crisps is what I'm served,
And I have to ask for French Fries, for chips I want reserved,
I ask to grill some bacon,
Whilst back bacon is pea meal I am told,
But the grill is called the broiler, as I stove I do behold,
Other things have got me confused on this trip,
A flashlight is a torch and a dumpster is a skip,
Garbage cans are dustbins,
Green fingers are green thumbs,
I ask for the city centre, go to downtown is what comes,
So go on vacation to an English speaking country,
But beware the English language, in Canada's kind of Funky

Reverie

Very early we lie in darkened room,
No one disturbs our reverie, our thoughts go round and round,
We lie there breathing deeply, relaxed and so at ease,
Whilst visions dance within our minds.
Of times that do us please,
Of friends long departed, gone from our domain,
A cavalcade of people, memories we can't explain,
In our minds eye they return, forgotten faces seem so near,
Whilst in this dreamlike state, our loved one reappear,
And all this wrought within our minds, with images so clear,
Reliving all those special times that gave us so much cheer,
We can create this montage, this video of times past,
Just close our eyes, relax and see,
What memories we've amassed,
Walk down this street of times gone by,
Drink this wine of silent thoughts,
And revel in this special place that our mind has wrought.

My son Robin rescued this cat that was being abused and took it home, after a time of distrust by Sparky a very special relationship was created which provided solace and comfort during a dark period of Robin's life. I wrote the poem for Robin when Sparky passed away.

Sparky

When you lose a close friend you are saddened,

It tears to the depth of your soul,

For memories you had of the good times

Do little to help our console,

Be it human or feline companion,

The bond that you shared was so strong,

So take heart in the memories of good times;

The sunlight of peace won't be long,

For it's knowing that you were a good friend,

Loyal and trusting and true,

Have no doubts as to how you're regarded

By people who really know you,

You helped when your cat needed helping,

And stayed true no matter the cost,

And despite the feline reluctance to aid,

You proved that your cause was not lost,

For when you yourself wanted comfort,

Curled up and on a bed laid,

A tabby cat with a crooked ear showed you comfort,

And at once came to your aid,

You both showed respect for each other,

And actions showed this to be true,

Sparky become part of the family,

Loved by your wife your children and you,

Sparky spent summers basking in sunshine,

Far from earlier cruelty and strife,

So the peace and protection you gave him,

Stayed to the end of his life.

On a walk with my granddaughter Iona, I was shown a special magical place where she informed me that fairy Tinkerbelle lived

Tinkerbelle's House

I know a magic fairy house,
Where Tinkerbelle the fairy dwells,
It lies deep within the woods
It's where she casts her fairy spells,
Its roof is a tree stump but inside you can see,
A little fairy palace, too small for you and me,
It has a door of oak wood and a knocker made of brass,
A Welcome sign upon the door so strangers will not pass,
For little fairy Tinkerbelle, will always welcome with a smile,
With dancing eyes that sparkle, that are sure will you beguile,
Come on in and have some cake,
It's made from woodland flower,
Have a cup of nettle tea and spend a pleasant hour,
And if you want to spend the night I have a room for you,
With an eiderdown of swansdown and a dressing table too,
So Iona next time you pass the fairy house,
In that very special place,
Be sure to wave and say hello with a big smile on your face.

Anyone who has a car can identify with this poem especially if the car is getting old.

The Joys of Motoring

A motor car it is the thing that gives us so much joy,
But I do believe that every car is like a spoilt child's toy,
Just when you think that all is well your mind is full of plans,
The little Grinch inside your car
Will scupper what you've planned,
The tax man he must have his cut
And raids your so slim wallet,
He wants a wad for road tax, its worse that Gastric Colic,
They make you buy insurance so you can safely ride,
But its nothing to what they screw you for,
When insurance quotes arrive,
Now happy as you drive your car down leafy country lanes,
But then you hear a funny noise,
You don't know what that means,
You try to just ignore it, but the engine starts to cough,
But alas the noise is still there when you turn the engine off,
Bonnet up you peer inside and look at all the bits,

You might as well give over,

As you don't know where things fit,

You ring the rescue services to cure your ailing car,

When they arrive you stand and wait,

And home seems very far,

The mechanic he pokes around and rattles bits of wire,

Sharp intake of his breath then says the prognosis it is dire,

You are towed off to a garage, your wallet starts to tremble,

Pound signs dance before your eyes as mechanics all assemble,

Your Credit Cards not flexible, debit card has had a stroke,

You stand there feeling pale and wan,

Your car has made you broke,

Oh! The joys of motoring, wind flying in your hair,

But that's a salesman's hogwash as you engine is laid bare,

Tired and broke you're sorted, you drive by limestone walls,

But then the Grinch it strikes again as a tyre pressure falls,

Oh! No this cannot be as you look at flattened tyre,

And trying to put some air in it makes you just perspire.

It's no good I will change the wheel,

But where is the spare one stored?

I'll have to find a jacking point I hope I've one on board,

Wheel changed were off again and arrive home rather late,

A happy day of motoring but I think I tempted fate.

The Fair

Can we go to the fair Dad, you know you said we could,
I've seen it down the end of street, and boy does it look good,
It's got a great Waltzer and a Ghost Train that looks scary,
Dodgem cars, and Wall of Death, that makes me kind of wary
There are lots and lots of sideshows, chips and burgers too,
A wonderland of promise for me and sister Sue,
I've saved up all my pennies in my tinplate money box,
And our Sue's got money hidden
In her drawer that's full of socks,
So all your brass it will be safe, resting there in your pocket,
As me and Sue will pay for rides on't great big twirling Rocket,
I know that all me mates will go, and Sue's girl friends as well,
And if we get up to mischief, Polly Green is sure to tell,
So as you see Dad, our bases they are covered,
With lots of new experiences, just waiting to be discovered.

Phone Call

When you don't hear that voice in the morning,

The day seems empty and bare,

It does not matter what you talk about,

It's just to know that your there,

We discuss what's been on the tele,

Or the latest book we've read,

And how kids are are driving us crazy,

With their antics and ideas in their heads,

I know that times are changing,

And the clock we cannot put back,

But its nice to have someone to talk to,

Some serious but mostly we laugh,

I just thought I'd tell you my feelings,

Regarding the use of the phone,

And I'm glad when I ring that I find you,

Sitting right next to the phone

Radio

Our wireless had an aerial and an earth wire in the ground,
With humming valves and lots of wires
So it could make a sound,
It only had two stations the Home and Light programme,
And through the war we listened, to these stations to a man,
We heard of Britain's triumph,
When the end of war's declared,
And the post war election when Labour's win was aired,
Our new Queen in the fifties was crowned and broadcast live,
And in many towns and cities, people listened,
Aa the ceremony came alive,
But when transistors came on track, it made the radio change,
And pirate radio also came which the "beeb"
Though very strange,
Small transistor radios and "ghetto blasters" came our way,
And radios got smaller as seen in present day,
We have all kinds of stations that cater for all tastes,
But now it's gone all digital, short wave has gone to waste,
We still enjoy the radio, the choice is never ending,
I really would like to know what changes now are pending.

Woodlands Song.

In a glade beside a stream,
Sits the woodland fairy queen,
A crown of moonbeams on her head,
In gown all stitched with gossamer thread,
With fairies dancing in a ring
Whilst a woodland elfin chorus sings,
To celebrate, sing and dance
With magic tunes that will entrance,
For midsummer's eve is the time,
That all the planets then align,
And magic flows midst flowers and trees,
As birds and insects feel the breeze,
That makes them sing and join the throng,
Of happy folk singing woodlands songs,

I cannot resist a challenge and when a friend said orange does not rhyme with anything,
I bet you could not write a verse about orange this is the result.

Orange

I was asked to do a poem, about orange by a friend,

It was the type of challenge that may beat me in the end,

We all know it is a colour and a juice we drink at meals,

As a child I did not see one, that I had to sit and peel,

Japan is full of blossom from the orange tree,

Which I know are pollinated by the busy industrious bee,

South Africa has a province that is Orange Free State by name,

It has a busy capital by the name of Bloemfontein,

The Orange River flows from Drakensberg to the sea,

And towns in the USA and France named Orange surprised me,

Holland has a Royal house with Orange as its name,

And William ruled in England a famous battle bears his name,

So with Curacao we raise a glass to toast poetic pride,

And with an Orange phone I show my brain I have applied.

Number 13

Thirteen is a number that gives some of us a chill
It makes some feel uneasy and some are even ill,
It's said to be un lucky, combined with Friday it is bad,
But a baker's dozen is thirteen, and the extra makes us glad,
A Celtic year has thirteen months, a fairy's year as well,
And both are very magical or so all pagans tell,
Twelve apostles at the table and Christ made it thirteen,
But Judas was a man who hatched a heinous scheme,
Twenty six letters in the alphabet but half is just thirteen,
And a suit of cards in a pack thirteen it's always been,
Thirteen pounds to work a week, seems now a meagre wage,
But when a child becomes a teen, he turns from child to sage,
At Bar Mitzvah in the Jewish Faith a boy becomes a man,
And thirteen is the given age when this ancient rite began,
If you want a game of Rugby League
Thirteen players is the rule,
But in Italy thirteen's not unlucky, and considered rather cool,
If you go to bonny Scotland the Devils Dozen is thirteen,
And thirteen famines in the bible disturbed the pastoral scene,
The first flag in America had thirteen stars and stripes,
But a coven of witches consists of thirteen different types,
The number has a history that spans the bygone ages,
And man's foolish superstitions
Is a thread throughout its pages.

As we get older and lose friends and family our thoughts turn to our own mortality.

Mortality

Another funeral to attend

Another farewell to say

As we our years increase

So do we recognise our own mortality

We see the mourners gather round

The tears so freely flowing

And hear the eulogy, of a life well spent

Whilst the priests voice intones

The riches of the afterlife

They are just words to those who mourn departed kin

Though meant to comfort

The words don't always touch their hearts,

They only think of loss and grief

And see a bleak future ahead

The final farewell said

A chapter closed

What does tomorrow hold?

This poem about light was written as an entry for a
competition and was exhibited in Bolton Central library

Light

The sunlight from the sky on high
Makes flowers and trees to grow,
Whilst light from a lantern shows,
The way, when the stars do glow,
It seems that light when amplified, can burn, cut and heal,
Whilst in a diamond, light makes its facets sparkle and appeal,
When light is dim and subdued we misinterpret what we see,
Which often causes anguish to the likes of you and me,
Sometimes when we're reading,
Facts are mixed up and confused,
But a light goes on inside our brain,
We no longer feel bemused,
Light playing on a prism shows a rainbow on a wall,
Which we see in the sky when light on rain does fall,
Our lives are regulated by the sun, all light at night does flee,
The light that shines in all our lives, is what other people see,
Light or dark it can be called our personality.

As the youngest child of my family with 2 sister one 10 years older than I and one 15 years older.
I "suffered" at the hands of my sister's such remarks as "have we got to take Him with us"
Still remain in my memory, I must admit I lingered when the boyfriend was around, it often resulted in me being given a few pence to go to the shops for some sweets!!

Mi Sister's Boyfriend

My sister's got a boyfriend and the house is upside down,

My mams all of a flutter and my dad just sits and frowns,

I can't get in the bathroom to go and clean mi teeth,

For she's always titivating, she's caused us so much grief,

I'm not allowed to play with toys,

'Case he should come and call,

Ma's polished up the hat stand and aspidistra in the hall,

We drink from cups and saucers now,

Dads not allowed to slurp,

No drinking from the saucer, and he's not allowed to burp,

She's gone and fettled up her hair, and has it piled on top,

Mi dad took one look at her and said it was a mop,

At this she got quite shirty and said he had no taste,

"I can still taste mi Sheppards pie,

But your hair looks a disgrace,"

Her face is full of war paint or so it seems to me,

With bright red lips and black marked eyes

It's a wonder she can see,

And her pointy bits they have enlarged

Her blouses seem much tighter,

She's high heeled shoes, and pencil skirts

And her hair shade is much lighter

Her boyfriend works at council, a calligrapher by trade,

That's a posh name for a clerk, it's all a big charade,

I want to get back to normal, so with my soldiers I can play,

I wish he'd go and marry her, and take her right away.

Alan a friend of mine is a golfing nut and is on the course rain or shine throughout the year this is dedicated to him.

Golfing Jeff

Jeffery Jones was full of moans his life was oh so dull,

His waistline was expanding and his spare time far from full,

A friend who'd got the golfing bug said come and play a round,

Join the local Golfing Club and your friendships will abound,

Now Jeff he was quite up to that, he thought it would be fun,

Chasing round the golf course instead of sitting on his bum,

His friend said buy some clubs, go and see the pro,

He'll fix you up in no time, and relieve you of some "dough"

Off he trotted to the shop; his dress at times was "loud"

He wanted to look smooth and sleek just like the golfing crowd,

He'd seen the golfers on TV, sleek pants and waddling rear,

Wearing hatched and checked sweaters,

Their panache to him was clear,

When kitted out with shoes and clubs

And a wheelie trolley too,

He headed out to the course, with a stop off at the loo,

To the first tee he did go with ball and tee in hand,

Looking down the fairway, he thought "by-gum" its grand,

With a flag stuck in far "greeny bit",

Near that bunker full of sand,

His friend said now address the ball, that to him seemed odd,

Do I call it Sir or Miss before hitting it with a club?

He thought he'd do a wiggle as seen by golfers on TV.

Then took a massive swing, the ball stayed on the tee,

He ended up in such a heap his posh pants stained with grass,

Looking at the un-hit ball whilst sitting on his ass,

Another three times he did try, but each one was a duff,

His ball was still immobile and he was in a huff,

Poor Jeff he took it badly as his partner gave a snigger,

He tried so hard to hit the ball,

But the hole he'd dug got bigger,

At last he hit the little ball and sliced it to the left,

Bounced in the rough a time or two,

Which made him quite bereft,

He hunted for a pleasant hour to find his errant ball,

Then at last he found it snuggly sitting in a hole,

He attacked it with a mashie, then a putter and a wood,

He moved the ball an inch or two

But his lie was none too good,

So far he'd taken twenty strokes, but he was resolute,

To get to that "flaggy greeny bit" his anguish was acute,

After another fifteen little hits he got the ball on't green,

A birdie, eagle, albatross, was nowhere to be seen,

He hit the ball it travelled true and popped into the hole,

And at once was eaten by a passing errant mole,

With seventeen holes left to play and night descending fast,

Jeff had played his first golf hole,

But I am sure it will be his last.

This poem which was commissioned to be read at the last service of a lady vicar who was moving on to take up an appointment in another parish.

Farewell

We say farewell to many things along the path we tread,
And parting from our trusted friends,
Fills some of us with dread,
But whilst we long for the security, of home and fireside chair,
We never know what challenges, we'll meet and have to bear,
But whilst we brave uncertainty,
Our friendships from times past,
Will guide and help us on our way, whilst we remain steadfast,
Saying goodbye is always hard especially when we're close,
And tears of parting cloud the eyes,
Of the ones who love us most,
So say farewell, adieu, goodbye, set your foot to pastures new,
Just be yourself and I am sure new friendships will ensue.

Halloween Night

The ghosts and ghouls are all flying,
To celebrate Halloween this year,
Off to the dark dismal castle,
To feast on wine, blood and beer,
The vampires have had their teeth sharpened,
To bite any neck that's around,
Whilst Zombies gather and stand there,
On strike so they don't make a sound,
Their very annoyed at the witches,
For a union they've formed don't you know,
But Zombies cannot be members,
For broomstick flying to them is no go,
The bats are out in their thousands,
Taking to the dim dismal air,
Enjoying the soft shadows of moonlight
And giving the occasional scare,
Count Dracula is the boss man, of the wizards,
Warlocks and crones,
And he's dining tonight in the castle,

On heart, sheep's liver and bones,

His goblet is filled to the brim,

With maid's blood and a whisper of gin,

So don't go out tonight or you neck he will bite,

And you will ever belong to him,

Now you know why Halloween's so scary,

And indoor you must always reside,

With cross, a stake and some garlic,

for protection if you do go outside.

I watched the Invictus games on TV and was moved to write this verse.

Invictus

Brave warriors who went to war at our government's behest,
Some were left with shattered limbs,
Minds anguished and distressed,
Tended by the Medic teams,
whilst their shattered bodies healed,
But in those dark satanic days, new terrors were revealed,
Was there hope in those dark days
That their lives were worth the pain?
And memories of comrades lost forever would remain,
And what of their loved ones, adapting to this blow,
Would they stay and support them? Or in their fear just go?
The Rehab teams got going to build a future that was bright,
But long days of sweat and anguish
Made some falter in that fight,
Was it worth the effort? My body's just a shell,
What have I got to offer? From this mind and body hell,
But change was wrought by skill and guts,
As learnt on fields of conflict,
I am Invictus was the cry no injury can restrict,
And so we see those Argonauts on another battlefield,
Display the passion, valour, pride all military do feel,
The sports field now their conflict zone,
Still fighting with such pride,
They show to all who watch them
That the Invictus spirit thrives.

A salute to the pilots who fought in the Battle of Britain in the dark days of the 2nd word war

With thanks to the Battle of Britain Pilots.

Looking up into the sky, I saw a lone plane flying by,
Its engine roared, propeller spun, the Spitfire ruled the sky,
Seventy five years ago a battle raged above,
Whilst young men fought the German foe,
Defending the land they love,
Hordes of enemy bombers flew to blast London and the Weald,
But pilots in their tiny planes, would never ever yield,
The Spitfire and the Hurricane forefront of Britain's might,
Took on the German fighter by day and in the night,
The sky above was filled, with the vapour trails of planes
And plunging aeroplanes on high,
Crashed to the earth in flames,
Young men, some in their teens, battled the deadly foe,
Some now lie in graveyards, midst crosses row on row,
The nation owes its gratitude,
To what Churchill called "The Few"
They saved us from invasion, by the jackbooted Nazi crew,
So when I see a spitfire, flying high up in the sky,
I think of all those gallant men some of whom did die,
Who gave their life for Britain, when its back was to the wall,
And even after all these years their exploits we extol.

This poem was written after attending a Remembrance Day service in Westhoughton Lancashire.

The Cross in Town

They came from every part of town and gathered round
That cross of stone, that special place,
Where to shed a tear was no disgrace
The young and old assembled there
To mark a time when war did rage.
The men in '14 went to war,
The trumpet sounds the guns did roar,
But in that sea of mud and gore
So many died, for what? They cried,
A generations young had died.
Since that war in '18 passed
Widows, veterans and the young,
Gather each year whilst hymns are sung,
We view the names inscribed thereon
But other wars have come and gone.
The wreaths of poppies they lay down
Have come from every part of town,
And folks remember ever year
Their sacrifice some shed a tear,
For father, son, or friend so dear.

Each year I write a Christmas poem the following odes are just a few of them.

Alberts Surprise.

It was Christmas Eve and old Albert the painter,
Was feeling all lonely and sad,
He'd seen no one for a week now,
And his relatives they were all dead,
He'd had a few lonely Christmases,
Since his dear wife was called to her rest,
But he'd always tried to be cheerful,
And did what he thought was fer't best,
He answered the door when a knocking was heard,
To disturb the silent night air,
And opening the door he saw Santa,
With his sleigh and reindeers out there,
Come in be welcome said Albert
And hutch up to the fire with thee chair
I've no fine wine in mi pantry,
But your welcome to cheese and some beer,
I know you are so very busy tonight,

Distributing children's presents and cheer,

Santa said I've come to give thee a present,

From all the past people you've known,

Who have told me all about you,

And how you'll spend Christmas alone,

In your life you've been kind to so many,

Some poor folk you've not charged at all,

When someone needed your guidance and help,

You never failed to answer their call,

So I've come to take you with me,

To visit your friends who gave me a ring

And they want to give you a Christmas filled,

With love and good cheer it will bring,

You're a good man Mr. Albert the painter,

You deserve what they've got in store.

For they just want to say a thank you,

For your big heart and so, very much more.

Christmas Markets.

Lights they twinkle on the stalls and people throng around,
Whilst traders stack stalls with gifts,
And jingling bells do sound,
Lights create a magic world, of fairy tale like splendour
People flock to the stalls, of the varied Christmas vendors,
One stall sells Christmas lights, another wooden sleighs,
All bedecked with fairy lights, around the doors and bays,
Children slowly saunter by with wonderment in their eyes
They see the Christmas tidings,
In stars that twinkle in the skies,
The baby Jesus lying there in the stable all forlorn,
A stall for a cradle, on that first Christmas morn,
Whilst carollers sing to passing crowds,
A joyous sound is heard,
That lifts the hearts of passers-by as they too sing the words
The Christmas markets are a time when celebrations in the air
A time of peace and harmony, a time of little care,
But remember that at Christmas time,
Some people have no homes,
And look to kindly people, to share a little of what they own,
Help someone who finds life hard,
Show them your Christmas joy,
And buy a little present for a less fortunate girl or boy.

Isolation

Her husband gently guides her, his face is worn and sad,
Now his wife's carer whom he married for good or bad,
She was his childhood sweetheart, and lived just up the street,
When wedding bells rang for them,
Their lives they thought complete
They had a child now flown the nest,
With children of her own,
But living oh so far away she keeps in touch by phone,
Her spouse never did the ironing,
Or washed the clothes or cooked,
His sweetheart wife of 50 years,
Ensured that naught was overlooked,
But in the last year things have changed,
These tasks are his work now,
Her mind no longer functions, for she does not now know how,
He helps her dress each morning, makes sure she has a wash,
And dusts and cleans,
So if folks call the place looks nice and posh,
At times she does not know him, a stranger in their home
He finds it hard to comprehend, he feels so on his own,
His house it is a prison, his friends all dead and gone,
But remembering his marriage vows, he cares and soldiers on.

Autumn Morning

You feel the chill. The morning mists lie across the fields,
The air is still, filled with night time dew soaked vapour,
Birds are silent in the trees,
Waiting for the sun to rise and clear away the mists,
Trees discarding leaves,
Turning the ground into a counterpane of many colours,
Whilst a watery sun rises slowly over the distant hills,
Migrating birds gather in increasing flocks,
Ready to journey to warmer climes,
Animals in forests scurry around,
Gathering the bounty of the harvest time,
Before they disappear to the dark recess of the earth,
To sleep away the winter cold,
This is the season of harvest and thankfulness,
For the bounty of the earth,
It seems so short as wind and rain,
Destroy the last vestiges of the summer past,
A last riot of colour
before the gaunt and sombre shades of winter,
Mask the Autumnal beauty of the fall.

A Christmas Message.

The tree is filled with baubles and carols fill the air,
The snow is softly falling in the midnight air,
Children are all sleeping dreaming of the morn,
Of presents and plum pudding
On the day that Christ was born,
But huddled in a corner away from the cruel winds sting,
A man was curled up sleeping, his coat is tied with string,
His possessions in a plastic, bag close by to where he lay,
A scene that's seen too often in the affluent world today,
But a person nears him bearing a cup of soup and bread
A blanket to wrap round him and a pillow for his head,
To invite him to a meal, shelter from the cold and damp
And to share some festive fellowship
Before on his way he'd tramp,
The fare it would be simple but the welcome would be true,
And the man's eyes filled with tears
after all that he'd been through,
He'd fought in France and Germany
When he was just eighteen,
Had a wife and raised 2 kids his life seemed all serene,
His wife she died the kids moved on and his job it disappeared,
His life it just imploded, his relationships all sheared,
But this simple act of kindness
When he thought that all was black
Showed him that someone cared enough
To help him to fight back,
The true Christmas message started in a manger all forlorn,
So help and share what you possess
On this blessed Christmas morn.

Birds

We see them wheeling in the sky,
Our feathered friends go flashing by,
The Swallow chasing flying midges
Dipping and weaving g under brick built bridges,
Whilst the Robin hopping on the ground
For seeds and grubs which in summer abound,
The Magpie's plumage black and white,
Could represent the day and night,
With one for sorrow two for joy,
Three for a girl and four for a boy,
A Kestrel nesting up on high
With speeding stoop, all seeing eye,
The night time patrol of the silent Owl,
Seeking mice or speeding vole,
We watch the Bluetit's feeding game,
Upside down on feeding frame,
The feral Pigeons always near
Looks for food with little fear,
Just a few of the birds we can see
Whilst relaxing with a cup of tea.

The local

I sit here in my local pub and look around the room
Sitting in the corner, it fills me with such gloom,
It's noisy and packed with folks enjoying a "quiet drink"
But looking round the folks that's in,
Has made me sit and think,
At one time in a pub you had, a room for men called Vault,
No females were allowed in there, a man's room to a fault,
They played their darts and dominos,
The language was profane,
In work clothes or their overalls, it was a man's domain,
No posh carpet on the floor 'cos beer was sometimes spilled,
Block flooring or dark lino was thought to fit the bill,
If you wanted to be quiet, or just to sit and think,
The Snug was just for you,
And if you had a girlfriend it welcomed her there too,
The lounge was where most people went,
Barmaids and chinking tills
Deep carpets, plush chairs and tables,
Water service, and drinks to cure all ills,

All the local characters you'd find standing round the bar,

Putting all the world to rights ,telling jokes from near or far,

The scandal of the neighbourhood

Was like dirty washing on display,

And who was sitting by the fire at home,

As their partners "played away",

Just ordinary people relaxing with their pint,

In quiet conversation,

In the local, Saturday night, their weekend recreation.

But now it's juke box blaring, or group singing on a stage,

The noise is quite deafening, talking's from a bygone age,

Folks don't drink mild or bitter, most drink larger cos it's cool

To me it tastes like water, from the local bathing pool,

Times have changed at the local pub,

Phone ring tones now abound,

The conversations stilted, when mobiles are around,

How can you talk on the mobile and to your friend as well?

I'd rather drink at home, away from that noisy hell.

Christmas Feast

It's here again, it's Christmas!,
The rush around has started,
Belt round shops as if possessed,
In search of toys and turkey breast,
Brussel sprouts and sausage meat,
Roasted spuds Oh! What a treat,
Must get some wine, and pudding too,
But at the checkout, what a queue!
And all this is for one manic day,
When we feast ourselves and later pay,
For all the extra inches put,
Upon our waistlines, Tut! Tut! Tut!
We all enjoy our Christmas splurge,
But Oh my God! The weight put on,
By eating Pud and vol-au-vent,
Indulging in a chocolate feast
And four mince pies at the very least
Our inches they have multiplied
By one or two or even five
All because we chose to say
We'll have a feast on Christmas Day!

Eagles

Perched high on craggy mountain top,

Midst rocks and purple heather

The eagle stands as sentinel despite inclement weather,

The eagles mate is ranging far in search of easy prey,

Soaring in the thermals of a cloudless springtime day,

This wild and savage landscape nature's forces has created,

Provides the perfect camouflage where eagles are located,

Their eyes forever moving, searching o'er the land

Among wild and lonely corries and the seashores golden sand,

These fearsome beasts of legend where hunted once by men,

But now they are protected on every loch and Ben,

We rejoice in their freedom

As we watch them swoop and glide,

The badge of Roman Legions

Which was carried with such pride,

Let's hope the Golden Eagle that some gamekeepers deride

Amidst the Glens of Scotland will forever there reside.

Dedicated to all my Scottish friends, who after a few wee drams, are inclined to tell tall stories.

The Haggis Hunt

There's a mysterious clan in the highlands,
McHaggis their tartan of choice,
For they have hunted the wild mountain Haggis,
Since they were all wee little boys,
They have honed their skills with the claymore,
Their sporrans are big wide and brown,
With lots of the silver dangly bits
Made by silversmiths of great renown,
The haggis is small black and rotund
With legs at the front and the back,
And it scurries about in the heather,
Wherever bad weather's on track,
It likes best the snows of the winter
When winds at a gale force do blow,
And hiding midst boulder and heather
Makes spotting them hard, don't you know?
The big hunts take place in the New Year,
When the Haggis Hunter's Guilds are in town,

Each hunter awash with the whisky
From first footing and the scotches they've downed,
Their eyesight at first is quite hazy,
And people in pairs they do see,
And spotting the wild mountain haggis,
Is a challenge on mountain and scree,
Wind under their sporran's a problem
A hot water bottle under their kilts all did put,
To keep them all sung and so warm like
So avoiding a frost bitten Butt!
They slowly crept up on the haggis
And cornered the brute near a wall,
But just as the posse were pouncing,
The haggis rolled into a ball,
Away down the hillside it trundled,
Followed by the McHaggis clan
But the bottles under kilts made them stumble,
And entwined with their legs as they ran
The hunters were soon in a big heap
And the haggis rolled far out of sight
So another year's hunt was a failure
Caused by supping whisky far into the night

Christmas time 2015 was when the North of England endured rainfall and catastrophic floods with damage to many properties.

Christmas Floods

Noah he was up in heaven he thought he'd have a lark,

I'll drown them northern moorlands, that'll do just for a start,

I'll have to get permission though, from 'yed Mon hereabouts,

I'll tell him folks bin naughty and deserve a great big clout,

They'll have to build some Arks like mine,

But not with plans from me,

Am afraid they'll have to scratch their heads,

And make their own you see,

But times have changed since Noah's day,

An' Northern folk are strong,

They don't build Arks any more, for sheep and cattle" pong"

It poured with rain in Lancashire and Yorkshire got a wetting

And rivers overflowed their banks,

And folks they started fretting,

They battled for their houses so people pulled together,

And showed that northern spirit, but prayed for fairer weather,

71

Northern grit will triumph

And Noah's plan could well backfire,

For when backs to wall and the going's tough,

Their courage will inspire,

Volunteers they came from near and far to lend a helping hand

To clean and sweep the houses

In this wet and rain soaked land,

Getting back to normal will take many days to right

But folk of Northern England will not give up the fight,

Let's hope the powers in London will plan to make them safe,

By the dredging of the rivers and put flood barriers in place,

So people in these northern lands

Can sleep safely in their homes

And not have to go a wading

When the local river decides to roam.

On seeing the local bus shelter torn to pieces by our resident mindless vandals I wrote this.

Vandals

In every town and village we have a little band,
Whose aim in life it seems to me, is to blight our blessed land,
If they see glass they smash it, a poster they destroy,
And painting tags on buildings, seems give them untold joy,
They have no social conscience, see naught beyond themselves,
They do not care for anyone, as their actions clearly tells,
Chastisement does not seem to work, it results in vile abuse,
And trees and plants that they destroy, continues that misuse,
If I went and vandalised their homes, as they love to do outside,
My actions would upset them, they would myself deride,
So what to do about vandals; remains a problem to be solved,
And I hope that police and public
Gets the matter soon resolved,
It seems to me that we should teach kids,
To value our fair land,
And not destroy their heritage,
whilst drugged up and half "canned"
The sanctions that we give them
Should involve some restitution,
To clean the mess that they have wrought,
As a means of absolution

All authors and poets have a writer's block at times so I decided to write a verse about this phenomenon.

Thought Block

I'm trying to write a poem but the words just will not come,
I've not even got a subject with which to write upon,
I rack my brains for answers to this monumental question,
But my brains given up its quest for words,
And gives not one suggestion,
I gaze around the room, and seek a means of inspiration,
But though I strain my brain cells, all I get is perspiration,
I've read the books on writing verse, preparation is the key,
But my brain has gone walk about, and deserted poor old me.
They say the muse will oft return in hours or even days,
I find that waiting's irksome,
In this word blindness kind of phase,
Oh please send me a sign, when normality returns,
So I can craft a poem which will voice my grave concerns,
It seems that I have done it with these few poetic lines
My thought block really fooled me,
I just misread my poor brains signs.

Spending.

My card is very poorly from spending so much cash,

I 'm feeling palpitations from shelling out my brass,

Oh why I was so foolish, why was I so rash?

My bank account is suffering from a massive drain of cash,

I've asked myself the questions do I want it. Is it vital?

Or is there anything I own whose purpose I can recycle

I now have to go and lie, in a darkened room,

To rid myself of dark, dark thoughts

That cause a sense of gloom,

I know that I have the cash and should not feel so low,

But spending money makes me ill and has since long ago,

Now it's time to loosen up and not take things to heart,

My spending spree has done me good,

So I'll make a brand new start,

No more to fret when spending cash,

No more that doom filled dread

I only need to worry when my account is in the red.

Mothering Sunday.

Its Mothering Sunday but no Mum is near,
To straighten tie or brush our hair,
For years ago she was called to rest,
A special Mum who I thought the best,
Its days like this that we recall
Those special traits which helped us all,
The patience, calm and loving smile,
The look that would at once beguile,
If we were anguished and afraid
She calmed our fears and made us brave,
Oh how I wish that she could see
That frightened child that used to be,
But by words and guidance we now display
The influences we espouse today
Our thanks to all the mums out there,
Who raised us all with kindness and care,
And let us hope that we do the same,
For all our children who bear our name

What's in a Name?

Oh Smith is such a common name
But shoeing horses was his game,
And Jones from Wales so common there,
Its Celtic roots now laid bare
But Fletcher's arrows flew straight and true,
Whilst dusty Miller ground grain for you,
Trelawney's name from Cornwall came,
And Gardener well you know his game,
McKay and Campbell Scots for sure,
With tartan trews and oh so dour,
And Irish Celts so full of Blarney,
The butt of jokes about Killarney,
So Brewer he controls the beer,
And Baker means an oven's near,
Singer is sure to hit the notes,
Whilst Shipman's on a boat that floats,
Garnet is a precious stone,
And Shepherd's make sure the sheep don't roam.
Now Fox is sly and oh so crafty,
And Hunt at times can be quite nasty,
Cooper he did barrels fashion
Whilst Taylor's stitched the cloth with passion,
You see your name can tell so much,
About our forebears, with the common touch.

My Granddaughter loves fairy's this is for her

Iona's Friend

Iona has a fairy friend she says

She comes from England

With clothes of pink and silver shoes

And a wand as sparkling as the dew

A Columbine bloom is her hat,

Iona says "now fancy that"

Iona watches as she dances round,

Her fairy ring on the ground,

She plays a flue like fairy Twig,

And dances to an Irish Jig

In moonlight she looks her best,

When little folk are all at rest,

But if you look in moonlights glow

Your special fairy she will know,

And give you a wave and smile,

Then you're off to dreamland for a while.

Robin one of my sons was a horticulturist for many years his pet hates were Garden Gnomes this is for him.

Wee Folk

They sit amidst the plants and shrubs,

And oft appear by planted tubs,

An army of friendly folk,

Who comments often do provoke,

One sits beside a garden pond,

His rod stretched out just like a wand,

I never see him catch a fish,

No doubt it's his undying wish,

Some people hate them, call them kitsch,

But those who love them smile at this glitch,

And amass these tiny little folk

To guard their gardens made bespoke,

These people who decorate their garden homes,

Are of course the Garden Gnomes.

Woodland Magic

We walked into this magic wood nearby a fairy glade,
And in a tree we saw a door that a carpenter had made,
It leads into a magic world of fairies, elves, and gnomes
Working hard to create for all, magic woodland homes,
A fairy queen and princesses ruled this secret land,
And kept them all from danger,
with spells wrought by their hands,
They had fairy dressmakers,
working with petals and with leaves,
And stitching them with thread
from spider's webs in house's eaves,
The fairy bakers made their cakes
And loaves from wheaten flour
And gathered nuts and berries from squirrels secret bower
The elves and gnomes they foraged far,
In boats on woodland streams
Their boats were made from tree bark
With Ash and oak wood beams,
So when you walk in nearby woods I'm sure that you will find
Magic fairy cottages in tree trunks just like mine,
But please do walk so carefully and do not make a sound,
Do not disturb the woodland folk
Who live in magic fairy grounds

Depression

Like a creeping mist over a moonless sea
My depression silently crept up on me,
I was so unaware, of the monster I was soon to bear,
My days took on a duller tone
I became sedentary and feared to roam,
Colours fade, the sparkle of the sunlight,
And the countryside, did not stir my soul,
I was wrapped in a cloak of solitude and despair,
Inertia gripped my very being,
I entered the Vale of Hopelessness,
My mind was numb, and life appeared to have no value,
People came spoke and went,
As though they were shadows in the night,
The Walls of Hopelessness surrounded me,
Stonewalls encased my being,
Looking up towards the sky.
I saw in my mind's eye only bars,
Which blocked my escape from my private hell.

Rain

I look to my window as I rise from my bed,
I look for the sunshine but I see rain instead,
It's rained for a fortnight and it swallowed up my lawn,
All the worms have lifebelts on
And it's covered with frogspawn
The willow tree is happy for water it doth like,
But the pigeons all have bathing caps to keep them dry at night,
My umbrella's over worked it cannot stand the strain
The spokes have all gone rusty in this unrelenting rain,
The milkman's float is very apt for that exactly what it does,
Its electric motor silenced, it does not even buzz,
He's stepped a mast with sail attached to carry out his rounds,
To all his rain soaked customers
Or those who have not drowned
The postman was a cheery soul before the deluge came,
But now he's wearing glasses
To read the rain soaked soggy names,
The police and fire and ambulances have all taken to canoes,
Their motive power all awash next to the Town Halls loos
The mayor has issued orders

That we must all grin and pull together

But he's alright in the town hall

Safe from the inclement weather,

The cheery weather forecaster

Predicts rain and sleet and snow,

To add to our misery when we are feeling low,

The rivers have gone walkabout into many people's homes,

And have created carnage drowning all the garden gnomes,

An air of melancholia has gripped this sceptred isle

All the people want is the rain to stop just for a little while

The fashion trends sou'westers welly boots and coloured macs,

We don't sing song about the sun for all we do is quack,

Climate change is all to blame the politicians say,

But all I want is to see the sun, Oh please, just for a day!

Finally my warped sense of humour is displayed in these last two poems.

Edgar Einstein

Edgar Einstein had a bot,
Which made a sound when he did trot,
It made him quite a unique guy,
Who never looked you in the eye,
For when walking down a crowded street,
His back chat greeted all he'd meet,
Which caused his friends to cross the road,
Whenever Edgar sort to rove,
The sounds and pongs has he walked by,
Caused dogs to follow and folks to shy,
So off to the doc's he did go, to stop his rear ends ghastly flow,
The doc pronounced 'twas most unique,
To have a rear that did speak
Inserted a bung to stop the flow,
Of all that emanated from below,
But alas this did not work,
The bung shot out whilst in a church,
The vicar had a nasty shock, his sermon flow it did stop,
Poor Edgar he was in despair,
Whilst making a hasty pant repair,
For now he's known both far and wide,
As the man who talks through his backside!

"Lucky" Smith

Lucky Smith walked down the street,
He crossed his fingers and his feet,
His walk was weird and most contorted
His life by superstition thwarted,
If your eyes crossed when him you met,
He'd cross the road running like a jet,
A rabbit's foot within each hand,
And horseshoes jangling on his waistband,
For four leaf clovers he'd search for hours
Midst flower beds and hidden bowers,
Whilst cracks in street he must avoid,
To step on one got him most annoyed,
Ladders he would never pass,
To walk under one would be his last,
On a 13th Friday he'd never roam,
Preferring just to stay at home,
He'd play all day with cards and runes,
And have a try at bending spoons,
His life and fate was his one concern
But fate then took a nasty turn,
For when walking down a local street,
Father Time he happened to meet,
A thunderbolt then struck him dead,
Despite his "lucky" cap on head,
Which goes to show that despite his charm,
Fate dealt a blow that did him harm

More Authors' From Violet Circle Publishing

Mike Beale.

Crumble's Adventures.   Children's Fiction.

Discover the wonderful world of Crumble, the little dog with a nose for friends and adventure. This delightful story is an ideal read for young children making their way into advanced reading, and also a wonderful story for mum and dad to read at bedtime.

Robin John Morgan.

Heirs to the Kingdom.   Fantasy Adventure Series.

A fast paced, action packed adventure set in the future after the world is devastated by a deadly virus, bringing about the end of modern life as we know it. Join a young boy who has an unnatural talent with a long bow, as he leads a group of his woodland dwelling friends against the might of the powerful Mason Knox.

This fantasy adventure takes threads of the past and weaves them into a modern, captivating, and thought provoking tale of the struggle of the woodland people, as they fight to preserve their life at peace within nature.

Ted Morgan.

Wordsmith's Wanderings.   Poetry And Rhymes.

Wordsmith's Wandering is a simple delight to read. Based on the life and observations of the author this reflective and at time very humours collection of poems and rhymes, reflect the 76 years of a man who has served in national service and the health system, whilst also working as a member of the mountain rescue team.

Colin Smith.

Heaven Knows I'm Miserable Now.   Stage Play

Is death really the end? Andy Reardon is about to find out, and he's beginning to wish it was. When Andy discovers his number is up, he finds the afterlife is not exactly fluffy clouds, harps, and Saint Peter.

What will Andy do about his dead wives?

He has three of them, all chomping at the bit to see Andy again but none of them are quite how Andy remembers. With Jesus Christ and Adolph Hitler dishing out advice, Andy might make the right decision, and be happy for all eternity. This black comedy takes Andy on the trip of a death time, and leaves him to make choices he'd never dream he would ever have to make.

Find out more about our authors, and their books at

www.violetcirclepublishing.co.uk

Violet Circle Publishing, Manchester, UK.

www.ingramcontent.com/pod-product-compliance
Lightning Source LLC
Chambersburg PA
CBHW071022080526
44587CB00015B/2463